The poems in Kim Sousa's *Always a Relic Never a Reliquary* draw from a wildly varied, continent-spanning, and consistently surprising lexicon. Political seriousness sits at the forefront of this work via (to name one of several threads) consistent anti-colonialist themes, yes, but there is also a clear synthesis of knowledge forms which fashions a singular, sensual poetic voice, with many poems grounded in inventive, visceral details of the tastes of foods, textures of skin and of touch, searing blood imageries, and much more. The results stick with you and demand re-reads. It is always a pleasure to spend time with poetry that is as embodied and risk-taking as this collection's.
—**Kyle Carerro Lopez**

The concept of the personal myth is introduced early in Kim Sousa's debut poetry collection. Recognition of this mythology and the ability to tap into its ritual, its prayer, and its power is necessary for someone who attempts to harmonize entire worlds in their writing. This is what Sousa does, and it is no easy feat. None of the worlds presented in these poems are the same. Few of them move toward or offer or demand the same things. Some exist only as spiritual masses, some are painfully tangible and sharply demarcated. There is the world of origin. The world lost. The world crumbling under violence and prejudice. The world containing only possibility. Sousa bravely traverses all of these and serves as their medium, their appraiser, their interrogator, their storyteller.
—**Gustavo Hernandez**

Kim Sousa's debut collection speaks on grief, prison abolition, and human migration. It is confessional poetry with teeth—teeth sharp enough to cut through the fabric of the American Dream and reveal some of the systematic horrors at its core. Like the poet, these poems "lean into rage" to help the reader confront the daily struggles that Black/Brown/immigrant people face in this country. Sousa's poems serve not only as witness, but as statement that we will persevere.
—**Nikolai Garcia**

Always a Relic
Never a Reliquary

Kim Sousa

www.blacklawrence.com

Executive Editor: Diane Goettel
Cover Design:
Cover Art: "The Blessing of Lazarus" by Rodríguez Calero
Book Design: Amy Freels

Copyright © 2022 Kim Sousa
ISBN: 978-1-62557-032-1

All rights reserved. Except for brief quotations in critical articles or reviews, no part of this book may be reproduced in any manner without prior written permission from the publisher: editors@blacklawrencepress.com

Published 2022 by Black Lawrence Press.
Printed in the United States.

*for every difficult body
across every migration*

In elegy

For the victims of State-sanctioned violence in detention facilities and at the hands of militarized police and CBP/ICE agents acting with impunity in cities across the U.S. For the indigenous people, activists and land stewards murdered by agents of Industry and State. For the Black Lives Matter activists in the U.S. who have been disappeared by the federal government in its ongoing derailment of Black liberation. For those lost to the carceral state. May we go on saying every name. No justice, no peace. Abolition now.

CONTENTS

Flood warning	1
Reliquary	2
If the neighbors seem friendly it's only because they assume we are the same	3
There is only grief	5
Poem for my immigrant father who has now left and will not come back	7
Watching "Lone Star Law" during the government shutdown over the border wall	9
Animals	10
My father knows what work is	11
Gemini Baby	13
Poem in which I go to three different grocery stores in search of azeite de dende, only to spend $9 on a jar at the health foods store	15
Poem about police violence	17
5-O Radio	18
Before the raids begin, I drive to work with a mango in my lap	20
Before the blood, I only know you through a screen	22
People say the world has always been breaking around us	23
Wire	28
Devotion	30
If I were to write my Latinx novel, I simply would not	31
My sister tells me the day I suffered a second-trimester miscarriage her friend was having an abortion procedure and invoked my name	33
To the white woman who thought a palo santo stick was a useless decorative object while her sisters drive the plant into extinction and The Amazon still burns	34
In which the poem always contains a shark and never a baby	36
Caracol	38
What wasn't gathered	40
I have nothing to show for my postpartum body	41
There are seven cactus spines inside my palms, and so I must be holy	42
Guilt I	43
Guilt II	44

The unhaunted poem	45
Yeah, I'm late to watching AHS 1984, but it's the night terrors of you making good on your promise to kill me that haunt me	47
Poem in which I try to eat flavorless soup at Panera and instead leave threatening to pull a gun on the white man who follows me to my car	49
Corpus Delicti	51
After your cousin won't let me hold the baby at the cookout	53

Here, again, grief fashioned in its cruelest translation:
my imagined you is all I have left of you.

from John Freeman's "Saudade"

FLOOD WARNING

It's always raining.
Sometimes, there's a comfort in this. Some personal myth
I draw from—that I was born in a thunderstorm.
That I was born at all.
This, some prayer card or candle.
Some small miracle I've already tapped.
My late period is here—even my body
has lost track of the days.
We are so tired, my body and I.
And still, we don't sleep. Shell and inside-shell.
Soft and once-was-soft. I am hardening with hunger.
I hold it in my hand like something saintly.
Part of rib. Piece of foreskin. Some proof
of life. I don't walk barefoot, but I did for a time.
My father and I, more alike than he knows.
I would light a candle at the altar
of his barefoot childhood. What is the prayer
for immigrant fathers? Why does my own poverty cut
him so deeply? I bleed from my ribs, too.
My life is staring at the blood-less stone.
I let the shower run over me on the floor of the tub. How to suture
self   to body?   What is the stitch?   How big the needle?
I navel gaze: too-hot water and skin red as hurt.
Once, the umbilical cord was everything I needed.
I was submerged and felt fine. Felt nothing at all.
Water-barrier.   Water-womb.   Link to the spirit world.
What whispers did I swallow there?

RELIQUARY

When I say house,
        I mean apartment. One bedroom. Low rent.
                When I say reliquary, I mean paper nest.

Strands of hair and feathers and soft
        plant stuff woven together by beak
                and talon. Spit-shined by wasps.

My home hums. Sometimes, the threat
        of swarm. But we are not wasps. Bumbling
                mosquito hawks, maybe. Circling each other.

Not mosquito, not mosquito eater.
        You have been misclassified.
                My *person not to possess*.

Here, in this almost-house, you hum
        loud as the crucifix, gold and bone.
                Loud as the pearl-handle switchblade.

The mods on the rifle.
        Inside, we wear no difference.
                Though there are hornets under your skin.

IF THE NEIGHBORS SEEM FRIENDLY IT'S ONLY BECAUSE THEY ASSUME WE ARE THE SAME

I move as one of them—with white
-skinned ease. Though I never learned to split

the difference between optimism and terrorism
enough for their fake flowers, their new year,

their allegiance to the flag. I walk on with my dogs.
They smell their same smells, kick up

more leaves, shit along invisible magnetic fields.
My compasses. I'm reaching for joy,

but can only land on proof of life: the cold sting
in my lungs, the still-up Christmas lights

—the dancing icicles most insistent of all. A sign
on the Brentwood Christian Church says,

WE ARE A BIBLE-BASED CHURCH.
I take this to mean interpreted literally—with none of the dark

and buried apocrypha. No promise of rest in desolation.
I want to keep walking past the library,

its more secular letterbox, but it's getting too windy.
The dogs have tired of kicking up leaves.

We'll have to turn back. Through the slot-and-dial
parking meters lining our way like optometrist's tests.

Here, everything is anachronism.
The open-air racism most of all—or not. There is no whole

without its part. I'm talking about this country, again.
Still, we walk towards some approximation

of home, to be shut in with the depression
of dirty dishes and The Reaper, her cloak a basement

-damp quilt of headlines. Complicit,
I put one joyless foot in front of the other.

I, vaccine-scarred South American, move
through this most "American" neighborhood,

crossing its redlined border
back to where I belong: into blight.

THERE IS ONLY GRIEF

shaped into another. The bath I draw
just to leave there, full. Surface unbroken.
The chickens outside screaming.
Nest-bound and raging
for the eggs that won't hatch.
My love on a bus.
Six men lynched.
My love says, *It's the pigs.*
You can't tell me it's not the pigs.
And I won't. When I say, I cannot
tell a lie, I mean, I'm rejecting white supremacy.
I mean it the way Arlo Guthrie said it—
even after his grandfather lynched
a mother and son. I cannot tell a lie.
There has never been an unsolved murder.
Maybe there was the impulse
to tell you what my love rides towards,
but it isn't mine to tell. Instead,
I kiss the flag he flies and burn the others.
Rub his body with a single egg
I crack into salted water and flush quickly.
Burning bay leaf love.
Boiled onion skin and white petal love.
I thought the egg would be black.
Too afraid to turn a smooth shell
against my own skin, I mop myself out
of the room. Floors Fabuloso slick
and shining my imposter face back at me.
My love says the sun can't burn us,
says our curls grow towards God.
I cannot tell a lie: passing
is a useless distinction. Here I am.
Even my father calls me branca—
though we do not speak.
His father broke the bottle

against my father's back
for the miscegenation.
My mother's family violence
didn't shine with blood and lamplight.
No, the whites disown quiet as a checkbook
balancing, an inheritance reaching back
into the pale. What is beyond this?
Not whiteness. But whiteness still.
I cannot tell a lie.
Look into my terrible face and know.
If you are what your father is,
my father said I couldn't be his.

POEM FOR MY IMMIGRANT FATHER WHO HAS NOW LEFT AND WILL NOT COME BACK

My mother and father are eating THE BEST FEIJÃO TROPEIRO!
at the small corner restaurant down the street from my grandmother's
—my VoVó's. I think of this boteco often.
Its cold-sweat Antarctica beers by the 600 ML bottle.
Its smoky skewered cheese cubes. And THE BEST! feijão tropeiro:
the black beans and fatty pork and collard green ribbons
and ground yucca root of my childhood.
Sometimes, I spoon the farinha into my mouth
from its jar in my Pittsburgh pantry—just to hold it there.
Dry, like the red dirt roads I walked barefoot.
I should be writing this poem in Portuguese,
but I never learned to. I am only literate across one hemisphere of this body.
My father says I was his impossible child: white-skinned,
blonde-haired, blue-eyed against mango trees, avocado trees,
trees I don't know the name of in English.
Trees that reach beyond translation.
Thicker canopies. Greener than. They planted one the day I was born:
difficult birth, small almost-tree, promise of some fruit.
Once, an avocado bigger than my child-heart fell
on our farm cat, and we didn't see her for days. Still, she turned up
—a little changed. Crooked where she wasn't before.
I remember the tamarindo tree at the end of our property,
the shotgun my father taught me to shoot at nothing in particular.
Towards the banana trees, maybe. To scare off thieves.
I loosened my grip on fearlessness in the United States.
Here, white is the color of fear. The color of all things.
I was sent to the principal's office constantly when we first immigrated.
Placed in ESL Kindergarten because no one understood
how easily I swallowed language, its mango peel slipperiness.
No one in Texas distinguished Portuguese from Spanish—Other is Other.
Five years old, white-brown and still unafraid.
How quickly you learn that to behave is to forget.
Still, I peeled the tamarind pods at the Mexican market hungrily,

stuffed them in my mouth with sticky fists, spat
the seeds onto tile floors under fluorescent bulbs. We grew nothing here.
Patchy strawberries in our rented backyard. Peppers, maybe.
Forgetting comes easily, now.
I remember my father's sweat, the way he could make anything work.
Sitting on the red roof tiles with him in Goiânia,
holding ladders in place for him in Austin.
I still dream in two tongues, but the dreams come less frequently.
My Portuguese is the clay oven my father stokes
in his new home in Pirenópolis: it burns slowly, warms some inner water.
He and my mother now live on The River of Souls.
Their neighbors bring horses by, help them press sugar cane
into caldo de cana on some oxidized old crank,
ask them to sign petitions; they write their way into their new lives
as water stewards. They will need to dig wells, buy milk cows,
carve out a cellar for the wine and cured meats they mean to make.
My father calls it a cave, has already found a place
with dirt that's just right in a way I don't wholly understand.
He tells me about the monkeys that steal their breakfast breads
from the kitchen, how he hasn't slept so well in as long as he can remember.
I know what he means—not since he left.
My mother tells me about the stars, how she'll need to find a map
of the Southern Hemisphere sky. She sends me pictures of the orchids
and staghorn ferns that grow unfussily from the trees.
The banded snakes that curl around their fence posts.
She has already bought cheese cloths, large clay pots and wooden spoons,
butcher's twine for making cheeses. Hung strings of peppers in the kitchen.
They will be poor, my father says. But his happiness betrays him.
Soon, we will have Catholic churches with no saints—
imagine that, he says. *There is no more dream of America.*
I tell my father I still light candles, though not in any church,
tell my mother to look for Crux, the Southern Cross:
a bird snare, a swarm of angry bees. A constellation small enough
to fit inside some inner jar, fill with tallow and dip into with a wick.
A candle you can carry across the wrong side of the equator.
A holy ghost.

WATCHING "LONE STAR LAW" DURING THE GOVERNMENT SHUTDOWN OVER THE BORDER WALL

Carmen pulls illegal "gill nets" from the Rio Grande, slices

      them halfway across the water.

                Let Mexico have their stuck and bloodied fish.

    Texas will keep its ruined half-net and absurd borders,   undone

by the river boat's motor, the struggling   carpfish and bluegills,

                Carmen's blade.

A border is only a catch-all. A bloody net.

    A faceless man across the water pulling you

      towards   the opposite shore—   even as you tear

reeds from the bank for an anchor.

     Your fingernails left in the mud like rosary beads.

Open your throat to the water: limitless,   sweet

                    and brown.

ANIMALS

To make a life, my father slept in hammocks in the park. For work, he cut
hunks of meat from a hanging carcass down to size. Always smaller, more precise.

Point to any part of the animal and my father can tell you its purpose. Its taste.
I remember boiling whole chickens, how feathers pull freely from still-hot flesh.

How to lay hunger bare: first, wring or slit a neck. Hold the pig's hind legs while
your father castrates the thing. When it grows to size, marvel at how clean a belly opens.

Later, we make soap from its warm wet squeals. We save its feet for the beans.
Its skin crackles in its own amber fat—still my favorite snack.

My hands haven't known animal blood on this side of the equator.
For this, I need to apologize. I hear it in my father's Texas backyard as the rooster

begins to crow into its sex. There is a stew pot waiting for its flesh. After a while,
we will break open its bones for their marrow. I will use my own capable hands.

Hands with my father's knotted knuckles. Our bones the same under my shame-white
skin. After a while, we will be full of animal. Its surprise cries for the sun.

We won't speak. There is a use and understanding in this.
There is thanks. A final sacrifice—less bloody than we expected, but bloody, still.

MY FATHER KNOWS WHAT WORK IS

Punching the clock at 5 AM, sure as he used to wake na chácara
to Dindinha roasting beans from green to black on the open fire—
What practical magic always had the coffee ready with the sun?
Only here, dentro dos estados unidos, we are being ground
between two stones. Pressed
for everything we have—and don't.
My father says he used to be the color of coffee.
His metaphor. Though, I've seen it.
Can there be an origin story for us?
I never ask through my violence of phenotypes.
White people have taken this from us, too:
tribalism. A red hat word. One that waits
to round us up at our work sites. For work or internment, both.
Our bodies, our bones. They would spill
every seed we carry.

        I easily pick my father out in old futebol photos;
          I remember the games.
       My sister and I—his impossible gringa daughters—
   with our baseball caps pulled tightly against the pigeon shit.
         That's what I remember. The pigeons.
     In the rafters like a coming storm: purple-black and loud.
    The beer-peanut-pigeon smell. Not my father on the field, driving
     forward towards the goalie, wearing out his knees for country,
       pushing his barefoot hunger behind him, always.
        My father! So casual about playing professionally.
    Throwing us on the back of the dirt bike as we screamed for him
    to send us flying over the quebra-molas, past the requisite traffic stops
    and police taking bribes, always mais rapido, mais alto to that grass field.
         No dirt to kick up into his eyes, finally.
          No patched and deflating ball.

If I learned what work is, it wasn't in the threadbare blanket
my mother saved from the flight that brought us here—
or in the wings the attendant stuck through me.

Not in my father sweating in restaurant kitchens, learning the word for knife.
Not assembling boxes at the meat packing plant on summer days,
holding his hand in the break room with its magic soda machine: what plenty!
No, work is sweaty and sucking ice chips, listening to his easy Spanish
with the others: three languages sprouting on my father's tongue
when the boss could only speak one. Pendejo / Porra!
What delight: to earn the worker's swears and contempt and calloused hands.
To eat the pickup truck oranges Dad sliced in the parking lot,
to watch the swipe of his knife against workpants
before he sprinkled each half with salt.
To stain my face and swallow each seed in secret.
In prayer.

                                                       For just one seed to sprout:

                                                                Little Alien

                                                              Foreign Body

                                                                 Migrant Thing

GEMINI BABY

I look for a dark line rising up from my pelvis to my breasts,
for any sign of you holier than the swelling. Not the weight of you, it isn't enough.
It's the end of the worst for us, Gemini Baby.
We're coming up on 12 weeks—that long exhale.
Soon, an ultrasound will confirm the due date.
But I am impatient. Has this been too easy? Hardly any sickness
and no blood—not even to mark your arrival.
You are now a lime. Almost plum. Tail-less, you shed the webs
between your fingers and toes. You breathe!
You are still see-through. Glass Lime Baby, we wonder
if there might be two of you. Tart-sweet citrus baby/ies, are there two heads?
You are a Gemini. We hope for two.
I want my dreams to tell me, but I can only dream of the end of the world.
Black Gemini Baby/ies, it is a broken window world.
I step on its glass again and again in my sleep.
You are growing your genitalia. I'm sorry. Baby They.
Know that, for me, it doesn't make you. I won't let it unmake you.
I don't want to know.
Gender Neutral Baby, what is there to reveal?
We still hold you close to our chests. Not quite a bluff baby,
it has been an easy first trimester. You grow sweet as the sugar cane
I will teach you to gnaw at the root.
But it has not been easy around us, our one body.
One man takes a knee for you, the rest would hang you.
There have been 307 mass shootings in the 311 days of this year.
How can I explain this, *Mass shooting?*
How can I keep the white men from you?
Bilingual Black Baby. Is that duality already enough, Gemini?
Immigrant mother, father on parole. All you will know is impossible love.
I will invoke the ancestors, call upon the healer-women
as I lower myself into the tub. A water birth to open the channel.
I pray a salt-rub rosary for my Great-Grandmother to visit us.
To guide the midwives' hands. She had a tonic for everything.
I rub a poultice across my belly. Against stretch marks and early birth.
Against whiteness, against racism's outstretched hands

waiting to catch you as I squat with the doula.
I am not blasphemous enough to hope for an easy birth.
There is already so much caught in my throat, and none of it feels like knowledge.
I want to call you Abelito, son of Mother Eve, first witch.
First woman to throw her man away.
How will we tend this garden, Gemini Baby?
It is a garden, still, even as we find bullets with our trowels.
We will unearth and lift high the skulls of our people.
Mine, a caravan moving like a dream in the desert. Blooming
from spilled canteens. Your father's: Black boys and men
with their hands up, their backs turned, falling to the ground.
But I will teach you the resurrection spell.
It's simpler than it seems: we say their names.
We unbury, bless and till the earth. We whisper in thanks to any green thing.
We must live here, Gemini Baby.
We must ground our feet in this soil, stained
as it is with our blood. We wear it in defiance, for protection.
You will come with spring.
You will be like a spring.

POEM IN WHICH I GO TO THREE DIFFERENT GROCERY STORES IN SEARCH OF AZEITE DE DENDE, ONLY TO SPEND $9 ON A JAR AT THE HEALTH FOODS STORE

The thing is, I know to buy Organic
to protect The Amazon, the pink river
dolphins that buoyed my fitful sleep
when my child mind still dreamed
in the place my body was no longer.
A coworker once asked me if
there are any cities in Brazil?
After she said the borough I lived in
was *pretty dark over there, isn't it?*
And I, idiot child who never learned
either of my countries' requisite
anti-Blackness, thought, *Sure.*
There aren't many streetlights in my alley.
Horrified to later realize she meant
my neighbors. The men who passed me plates
off the grill, helped me heave a curbside
armchair into my walk-up, said,
If you need anything, Baby.
And then, my roommate. In another apartment,
now in a white neighborhood, who said,
I just think it's funny that your dad
grew up in a favela. And he didn't?
We are poor, yes—but country poor.
My father was lost in the jungle,
not stacked-high concrete.
Not City of God but Stay With God.
It's the only story my father tells. Me, anyway.
And if I've stopped waiting for a father's stories,
I've stopped waiting for a country or a race.
Unclaimed thing, I spat in the face

of a woman who looked at me and assumed
I would accept her slurs.
I am kin to no "American."
North, South. What they ask me
to pledge allegiance to, I do not.
What is *order* and *progress*
when the state measured each
by the erasure of Blackness and Indigeneity?
What terrible math made me?
Exhausted, I buy the overpriced red palm oil,
close my eyes too long trying to name it in English
when I ask for help finding it on the shelves
of olive and sunflower and corn.
What am I looking for, again?
A place? No. Not exile. A flavor profile. An ancestor.
Peixada isn't even our tradition. None of us fisherman.
Peasants, farmers, cooks. Calloused and cursing, cursed.
What is inheritance if not another shadow
of colonialism? This, I won't stitch to me.
Instead, I will make the stew as a talisman
against the ghosts. Or, as their offering.
If my love were here, he would offer up his arms,
say, *I'm going to save y'all.*
All of my father's children, lightening
with our country's violence.
The ancestors' scowls in every photo.
Their brown eyes to my green.
People size me up, solve the equation too neatly.
Say, I chose, could unchoose who I love.
Maybe. But I could never choose the mirror.
My love says, *There's really going to be a Brazilian me.*
And how can I show him? How can I tell him?
If he is Home, he would be, our son would be
more at home in mine than me.

POEM ABOUT POLICE VIOLENCE

      after, with lines from June Jordan

I panic-wake to too many missed texts:
I'm enraged, he starts. My love speaks always
in two Cs, curling back on themselves like a trigger pull,
a handshake hooked on Community Revolution In Progress.
I want to say the day burns before it blues,
but what use is that? Cobalt will have you crazy
in a cornfield, we already know.
My phone screen is still the precinct on fire,
a Black fist, a middle finger raised, rising like a new anthem.
A ringing in my ears. The absence of a flag—finally.
tell me something / what you think would happen if
I think of driving to Portland to light a match.
Instead, I send my love June Jordan.
every time they kill a black boy / then we
What does it mean to sit in silence
when we are both so loud? *Sometimes the feeling*
like amaze me baby / comes back to my mouth and I am quiet.
Sometimes, I slit open a fish
from ass to chin, separate the gills
from its head and pull.
every time they kill a black man / then we
It would be that easy.
you think the accident rate would lower / subsequently?

That heaven was a bowl was only a mistranslation:
God's bowels open above us.

Where there are stars there are entrails.
I run red hands under water.

Sometimes the feeling like amaze me baby.

5-O RADIO

It starts harmlessly:
an abandoned backpack a white male eventually comes back for.
No mention of the bomb squad. No panic.
They speak in numbers and static. I worry they can hear us.
You play too much, pretend radio back: *Over. Out.*
If the U.S. is a terror or surveillance state,
you're on the side of surveillance. And I, terror.
Unmanned drone strikes and Dad calling about My Documents again.
Disappeared Black activists and The Wall. White people everywhere.
Their trust in police chokes like an algae.
On the scanner: police chase an intoxicated driver through our neighborhood.
Intoxicated. As in, needle, bottle or both. I bring up that bumper sticker
I see on pickups with confederate flags and dangling testicles:
SAVE AN ADDICT SHOOT A DEALER.
An invitation to a lynching and more static.
I feed the dogs salt and pepper potato chips, watch them *crunch crunch*
and beg for more, always trusting more will come.
Let me live for a while in this dog-faith.
Let me trust the hand reaching towards me.
When I run out of potato chips, the dogs lick my hands.
Is it that white people live a life without salt? Would that they would bloat
and float away across the ocean. Let them be the raft, one time.
Suddenly, *Black Male. Black male in a red white and blue coat with fur trim.*
We are struck. No. Stuck. These are the facts:
A Black man tries to sell a bus pass at the bus depot downtown.
A white person feels uncomfortable. The cops are called. We hold our breath.
After dark, we let off shots for Antwon Rose. It isn't any kind of answer,
but it feels good to lean into rage.
Unlike the courts, we will put a name to this.
Our nose hairs sting, hands blacked by powder. But we are steady.
It's about breath, shooting.
All I know to pray for is strength: let me be powerful.
My hubris: with this gun, I am ready for the race war.
Let La Migra try me.
A bullet is only a seed unburied. And I was born to till this earth.

Green thumb and trigger finger.
I will not be so polite about the borders I draw.
I will take back every avocado, peel the mango from white hands
the only way I know—with my teeth.
Imagine, only knowing unripe fruit.
I will not be bruised by plodding thumbs.
In Brazil, if you bite into a seed expect the thorns.
I have a blade and whetstone for every tongue.

BEFORE THE RAIDS BEGIN, I DRIVE TO WORK WITH A MANGO IN MY LAP

    1.

I drive to work with a mango in my lap like a green lung
collapsing, my grandfather weaving palm fronds
into rooves as The Amazon burns.
I peel the mango with my teeth—old and sacred habit—
spill its yellow from mouth to womb. I spit the mango's red rubber skin
into white neighborhood after white neighborhood:
I invite rot as reparations for their hard red lines.
Earthworms migrate deeper darker, swollen with rain and blind to borders.
And the millipede and beetle grub move this earth—what of it is left.
What can we abolish that they aren't already at work composting?

    2.

I would wear the mango around my neck like a figa: for luck, for country.
But a mango is a thing you can gift yourself, ignoring
the woman at the checkout counter who asks if you're trying to decide
which you like best: ataulfo or Tommy Atkins/Haden—
the latter mangoes I have to Google to name. All fiber and long shelf life.
Named for white men in Florida. Really, any other mango would do.
And what the fuck is a champagne mango, anyway? A white mouth
refusing to open for syrupy vowel sounds. A violence
like white hands in wet soil. Their teeth clapping with consonants.
Always *dirt*—never marga, argila, barro.
What they keep they kept from us: our gods, seeds and sweetness.
My father says he wouldn't even feed the mangoes we settle for in the U.S.
to the pigs in Brazil awaiting his homecoming.

3.

I drive to work with the mango pit between my teeth like a blade.
I am nectar-stained panic: mammal, *animal*.
Red light. They will come for us. Green light. This is promised.
Yellow light. Even as we are drowning in the swollen rivers,
they bare their teeth like 32 white colonies and call it a smile.
Already, they are coming for us, having sliced
open their own palms to pull the pits from our avocados,
thin lips rashy from our mango skins.
Always, Once, or Still, white men sell human fat as a delicacy.
From guillotine to gut.
Are these the ancestors they will call upon when the sirens sound?
No, there will be no sirens.
Already, the silence.
They will spill out of white vans in riot gear, AK-47s ready at our spines.
And still, the silence. They will do it in the daylight,
though their skin will burn. And we, interred. Encamped.
Too sick to rattle our cages—too young and dying.
Too old and deported [sic] *Removed*.
Every mango left heavy on the branch. Every branch breaking.
Yes, I will plant this pit—sure as it will not sprout.
Sure as the soil will open wide her stateless mouth to receive it.

BEFORE THE BLOOD, I ONLY KNOW YOU THROUGH A SCREEN

Obsessed, I look at the graphic at 6 weeks: little bean sprout.
I pull up the app again. Hello, salamander. Seed. Suspicion.
I watch it float in my phone screen womb. I try to zoom.
I scroll into Week 7, Week 8, Week 9. It shapeshifts.
Still, it floats.
Hello, limbs. Hello, ears. Hello, kidneys.
I cry at the overwhelming cruelty of subjecting women
to an ultrasound before an abortion.
I dry-heave. Again.
Here I am, so careful not to name the thing *fetus*.
So overwhelmed by a graphic.
A rendering. Trick of some algorithm.
And I have been tricked.
I open the app. I open the app. I open the app.
Little almost-heart: already, you beat 150 beats/minute.
I have already once bled you and been wrecked.
I know the infinite and varied ways a body betrays.
Little kumquat, I know that you will be as Black as I am white.
Here, in this country with so little imagination.
Even my repatriated father forgets:
it's The Américas—not "America."
In Brazil, they say being Black in the United States
is like cacao. Split,
fermented and unsweet.
As if that metaphor were at all anti-racist.
As if racism knows any border.
As if Triangle Trade didn't hit us hardest.
My ironic countrymen, their Black Madonna
and their anti-Blackness.
Still, Querido, I whisper to you in Portuguese.
You, a pin drop.
A terrible hope.

PEOPLE SAY THE WORLD HAS ALWAYS BEEN BREAKING AROUND US

The story goes
my father hired coyotes
in a custody dispute.
Who is left to say if this is true?
No one here.

Still, men like my father fold
too much trust in oxygen,
the coyote's sun-up yawn.
Neither can swallow
an imaginary line.

How can a train be a beast
when no white man will slaughter it,
leaving us to starve
and it belly-up and wasted
on red hills?

Chance swells the rivers.
To survive The Desert,
cut open a cactus, move inside
with the owls. Its spined arms open
like a grandfather's ghost.

Lick clean the wet sponge insides:
the only water what it pulls
from the ground. Sleep.
Soon, the bats. Flowers
open for the green-gray moon

indistinguishable from paper
moths like slow-motion fists.
The lizard's blue tongue
is an omen. Sew yourself
inside the cactus.

Each suture
a drowning.
Each drowning
a howl, crack
of heat lightning.

Liberty a mirage.
Spilled canteen.
Spilling tanker.
Beautiful oil slick.
Beautiful ocean.

A lung capacity
for both, but above all
for sinking.
If I have always
been *animal,*

how is it that I only now file
my nails into incisors?
Yes, I still write poems
and eat chili mango at my desk.
But every poem is a container

for the gun
I know to aim
at their necks, exposed
in spite of their armor.
Bad imitation

of the sacred armadillo.
Look for its crossing
before you make yours.
Hold tight
to yourself.

Let the pale militias march.
Let them aim for kneecaps
and find only brown dunes.
Mother Desert will not abide
her buzzards

to carry cowards
into ascension.
Her sands
will not swallow
their bones.

And though The Rebel From Nazareth
said to wet mine enemies' lips,
I'd sooner take the automatic
Felony Murder for shots fired
above their shoulders.

A wound
is only a waste.
You can only dance
around the dead.
Already, I've practice-shot

the opossum
on the fencepost,
the broken horse,
the shadow
that cried like a man.

See, a moving target
leaves less room for remorse.
All I know of bloodlust
I know because my father
has seen the panther

lit by lightning flash,
its padded feet keeping pace
alongside him in the jungle.
You can't unrun what's intent
on moving inside you:

our line possessed
by amber eyes
and plasma-wet mouth.
Its hunger our legacy,
the mask we wear.

Nights, I tear
at the sheets like flesh.
I peel clothes away
from my summer-sweat lover,
sleep on his smoker's chest, rattling

like the sound of coming drones.
But our sleep is shallow.
We leave the police scanners
on, our emergency contacts up.
I input my loved ones into an app

as part of my Preparedness Plan
I can Deploy with a fingerprint:
*Hello, I think I'm about
to have an interaction with deportation agents,
and I'm at risk of being detained.*

I listen for the raids
because in the end,
citizenship will not matter.
Already, it doesn't matter.
I am running out of safe crossings.

And my father: on some watchlist
in spite of his green card.
Their marriage, my mother's whiteness
will not save us.
When a stranger asks,

What's your story?
Where are you from?
I do not answer.
The smell of lye still strong
in my nostrils.

My nails still scrubbed
so clean they scream.
It's hard to burn
what's blood-soaked:
evidence, this country.

Better to bury it.

WIRE

in response to the recent exaltation of barbed wire
by the fascist 45th president of the United States
and a certain best-selling novel

We used it to keep the cows out—
or in line. A fence: for vaccines, for dewormer;
to cut a single notch in each velvet ear
when we thought a brand too cruel;
to reach inside mother for calf.
Thick-coated thing. I loved every one,
its reaching tongue wrapped around my child-wrist.
The warm ready udder against my palm.
What kind of unity exists apart from this?
A country can't know or claim it.
Still wet from her labor, I stomped through termite mounds,
ran with bees in my hair, not stinging but stinking.
The tamarindo tree was The End,
but the land kept growing. Tumbling
into someone else's bananas.
Of all the trees, a banana's thirst is most insistent.
And so, it walks farthest, fastest.
Its heart hangs heaviest in oxblood drops.
Somewhere, an old man kept honeybees
in gourds, a perfect perimeter around his house.
Four mud walls, humming and sweet.
When I say kept, I mean invited in.
My father doesn't remember this old man.
Only a ghost hand in the yucca leaves
warning him to go. A vision of unbelonging.
It wasn't our land, he says.
His own father buried, though I couldn't tell you where.
Sent down the river or led across
by someone more forgiving than Death.
What we once believed walks on
without us, turns to look us in the face
and doesn't know, will not claim us.

Still, we hear it in the street dog's howl:
a path to the other side.
One we won't find in this life.
This is the only crossing, unbarbed.
Unmuddied. The Carpenter walked
on bloated water—or water that bloats.
Water can be beautiful.
A body, too.
All of us mud and rib and riverbank.
But never wire.
Cursed corona, it cut
even The Carpenter's head.
And when He rose,
He found it teething
at His still-beating heart.

DEVOTION

My grandmother blesses her plants with holy water
and us with their wet soil. Even the ants in her house
follow Christ in their marching: here, work is holy.
And God was a man with calloused hands.
If o que os olhos não vêem, o coração não sente,
there is nothing I don't see: the ghost-dogs silhouetted
beneath the mango tree on my Vó Eva's red dirt city street,
my Tio Fábio always sweeping away the dirt, strays.
Unloved and nameless things always return
like hunger: o melhor tempero. The best seasoning.
And dirt does the work of keeping the dead.
We light candles for The Trinity and our ancestors.
We offer shots of cachaça to faces I'll never recognize
and my father doesn't talk about.
How holy a wound: our displacement in the United States.
My father, his own blood a devotion.
We take a shot: Saúde. Prosperidade. Felicidade. To us.
On Fridays, we wear white. All faith and superstition, possessed
by what my grandmother believes in.
And the strays, again,
nosing at mango pits and garbage bags, whining through the night.
And the quick flash of pistol a neighbor shoots through veranda bars,
the scattered silence of a heartbeat just-missed,
my VoVó ushering me into the house and making the sign of the cross,
putting me to bed under Jesus' sacred heart, burning
and lanced, bloodied and ringed by thorns.
He holds us in His wounded palms: a refuge. A refugee.

IF I WERE TO WRITE MY LATINX NOVEL, I SIMPLY WOULD NOT

Leave prose to those without rage
and ADHD and prescription lenses that double
down on themselves every year. Each eye rock-em-sock-em
robotting the other. Yes, my vision narrows
like the poem. Cutting away, cutting
away. My grandmother's eyes scraped clean
by lasers again and again. My dogs going blind.
Their mutant eyes too big or too kind.
Still, they sniff me out. Submit
to whatever instinct has escaped their breeding,
human selection. There is no way to be precise
or concise about this, and yet, here we are.
My skin is white; my sister's brown.
An anomaly: my violent phenotypes.
Itself a mutation—a mother's cursed privilege
first appearing in a single individual
only 7,000 years ago.
And yet, only her daughters'
migrations could be borderless.
Today, their every plane ride is a conquest.
Every sunset selfie spit in the eye
of every mother who will never be reunited
with her now-trafficked child.
Reunification is no antonym for *removal*
when both call for a cage.
I learn too late my Dindinha had blue eyes.
Though not for the reason you think.
She walked between worlds.
Salt and herb woman, she ate with her hands,
refused the colonizer's tools, baked peanut cakes
in tins emptied of their salted fish,
said what is given is enough.
Not haunted, but a haunt,

she comes to me as a blue orb, suspended
long enough to capture on film.
A terrestrial gray cat with blue eyes,
she gifts me my familiar and disappears.
If this is her pardon, I don't want it.
Still, my forest spirit gathers acorns in the light,
keeps my sleep at night, his purrs a tether
to a realm I didn't ask for, but received.
How could I dance across a border when my skin keeps it?
Solve for the science that says there is no gene for this—
inheriting or wearing the ghost. Only an absence
of proteins, the sun, equator.
A diet changed by the shuttering
of The Garden gate. The first gift
was not The Word, but what we took for ourselves:
terror. Not apple but pomegranate,
not knowledge but self-consciousness.
A rind I cannot peel away,
the always-awareness of a bloody fruit.

MY SISTER TELLS ME THE DAY I SUFFERED A SECOND-TRIMESTER MISCARRIAGE HER FRIEND WAS HAVING AN ABORTION PROCEDURE AND INVOKED MY NAME

This friend (yes, she is)
I have never met, will never meet, told her,
I felt like your sister was in the room with me.
I felt like she was telling me it was okay.
Stranger,
let's put aside your rights, mine.
(Though yours are guaranteed and—)
Though I have astral projected
in this only on-forever life,
it was not that day in that room.
And though our pain has, historically
speaking, been a profit-
sharing program for your people,
you cannot invoke my name
when you can't pronounce it.

TO THE WHITE WOMAN WHO THOUGHT A PALO SANTO STICK WAS A USELESS DECORATIVE OBJECT WHILE HER SISTERS DRIVE THE PLANT INTO EXTINCTION AND THE AMAZON STILL BURNS

Yes, I guess it's ironic that Paulo Paulino Guajajara was shot
dead in an ambush by loggers one week ago.
Everything's ironic to you people, isn't it?
A sacred plant, a forest steward, a bullet in the brain.
The match strike, most of all.
My father named my brother after Chief Raoni Metuktiri,
but voted in Bolsonaro. A black smoke irony.
He says it's Our Fascist President's detractors
setting the fires—not his policies
against every thick-trunked ancestor still rooted
in the damp. Their still-reaching canopies.
Against this earth's original peoples—you forgot,
I know. There are people in The Amazon.
My grandfather, now only ghost, moving deeper into the forest,
farther out of my father's mention.
All I know is his name, its own ironic violence: he who is without sadness.
In a photograph red as the water, he holds my father under one arm,
my Tio Fábio under the other, splashing in that great river.
But that's not for you—
it's hardly for me. I myself a ghost
in my grandfather's eyes: white-skinned, unclaimed.
Some gente still claim mestiz* in this, The Year of Our Lord Ablaze.
Nossa Senhora, I am complicit and irresponsible enough!
My brother, Catholic, dutiful,
will name his baby Gustavo, protected by God.
He asks if I can pronounce this—
I don't list the tongue trills I had ready for my baby, Little Never-Was.
Fire-Gone-Out. Nights, my skeleton dances
above me: my hips shake off the blood. Still-widening

to fill the room. Castor oil and cocoa butter irony.
Stretch marks and childlessness and soil erosion.
The West was only cracked in two after the Holocaust—
not after its smack-jaw Colonialism,
its Chattel Slavery that stained even the water.
So your Post-Modernism tells us, anyway.
Your art is white supremacy, I'm sorry to tell you.
No, I live to tell you:
this country is only a name
for every other genocide it won't Proper Noun.
What pill is there to swallow against this?
The anti-depressants aren't working:
there is no way to distinguish clearcutting trees
from clearcutting bodies.
Recalibrating my reuptake inhibitors now.
What you can and can't tell your pharmacist
is what you can and can't tell your lover.
I'll never say I see things.
The coyote with a rabbit in its jaws in every parking lot.
This country: all parking lots and The Seventh Cavalry opening fire.
The irony. Declaring The Badlands public land.
Setting fire to anything but ourselves.

IN WHICH THE POEM ALWAYS CONTAINS A SHARK AND NEVER A BABY

A friend came to visit and said I was only *expressing cells*—
and the white doctors, too: *a body has a way of taking care of these things.*
How I cried in spite of the morphine drip. How the contractions came
and never stopped coming—which is to say it felt
like they would never stop coming—
until I was no longer a container but a comma
curled in on myself against the bed rail, still white-knuckled
with such unfamiliar pain. Even as I fell away from the room and tore
out the IV, the nurse insisted, *No, you never lost consciousness.*
And sent me to walk across the floor without those mesh panties,
so that I left a trail of blood behind me for whatever spirit to follow.
And the ultrasound tech with that not-dildo and her cold hands.
How she spat in disgust at *the mess* she *had to clean* wiping me down,
wiping me down. I wore the bloody gown home—
what other choice was there, every choice having been taken from me, already—
home to where the toilet was still covered in blood, mine
and not mine. Paloma's or Joaquim's.
Because my thinking mind understood that inside me was only a fetus,
but my body, my blood was already Mother—
through the first trimester and swollen with affection and future possibilities.
A love gripped by fear—that I now know was intuition—
reaching inside myself anytime I felt wet to make sure it wasn't blood.
And when it was blood—ER Visit One—
I hadn't even suspected, was only wiping myself on the toilet at work.
Had I not prayed enough? Had I not lit every candle?
The nurse, the doctor, said *it's nothing, it's nothing* even as there was nothing
on the ultrasound. Only the sounds of my own washing machine insides,
my own arrhythmic heart. How my blood pressure went tachy
at every insistence to *be calm*. Just as it was my rapist who told me to *relax*.
How can I explain the missing time? Maybe the alien abduction
I prayed for as a child, the hope for ascension into a mothership,
was a vision of my grief, of every time I have stepped outside of myself
and climbed higher—but never high enough.

I could never escape the hands inside me I didn't ask for.
Missing time suggests the presence of another, static from another realm.
So maybe I was not alone in that cold room
and Paloma or Joaquim was carried through the curtain
and across the river by some ancestor—but then, I didn't make a child, did I?
Not even an infant, only a dark, unknowable mass.
Like the marbles I used to peer into for crystal balls as a child—
always hazy. Better to shoot them into the pile.
Like the Gulf, which never presented the shark fin
I had seen so clearly in dreams—not until my sister caught
that juvenile bonnethead deep sea fishing in Galveston.
We made peixada with shark meat and buried the hacked head
in the backyard, my sister hoping for the thing's open jaws for a trophy.
Only, when we dug it up, it wasn't picked clean
by whatever slept under the earth, but swallowed by it.
Disappeared. Nothing remained but a complicated sadness—
because inside sadness you can arrive at relief.
To not have to look the thing you've buried in the face,
to not have to bury the thing at all. To stop grieving a soul
when all along there was only

blood.

CARACOL

You were the size of one of the snails I used to race
in Tio Pedro's backyard. Raised like livestock in miniature
in a small wooden hutch. Here, I made a hutch for you,
split it from myself:

                a uterine sac.

The doctors insist, but I cannot be blameless in this.
I have pulled snails from their shells and run them through herbed butter.
I've sopped them up with crusty bread. Alone in France,
trying to shape my loneliness into something fashionable—an aperitif.

Home in Brazil, I have broken
so many chicken necks, plucked so many feathers, seen the cuy

      split open, stuck through
         and flattened onto spits at the feira. I might reach for a papaya, instead,

                but the gaze has its own appetites.

They would not call yours a death, Little Snail.
Instead, a loss.

      I could not keep you.

Now, a pain pill lulls me to sleep.
The curtain between us   flutters

                somewhere out of reach.

      Go / Stay.

If life does not begin at conception, death does.

                                                  I made a death.

I am the screaming steam loosening flesh from spiral shell.

I follow, cloaked in my grief.

                                                  I am the scythe.

                                                  Unwitting blade.

WHAT WASN'T GATHERED

How much possibility can we let go of
and still celebrate the slice of honey comb,
the soft persimmon, the unclotted cream?
I'm finding it harder to feed myself
when it has always been so hard. Body,
it was the baby that finally broke me.
This uterus a somehow-hollow
that still refuses to shrink, even as I do.
It was only *baby* to me, in the end. *Fetus* to all the others.
The loss an unknowable thing I still must answer:
How many times has Jesus' face appeared in the clouds?
How many lemmings did scientists throw from how many cliffs?
How does the soul leave the body?
My mother says, *But you didn't,* when I try to talk about the contractions.
That unproductive pain. *But you didn't have contractions.*
You didn't go through it for twenty-something hours.
I fold my twenty-something arms around myself.
These only arms. Yes, I ruined my mother's body.
She told me again and again.
I can apologize in more languages than I understand.
I kept her in labor for an entire day, fighting
my own entry. Strangling myself blue.
Mine, a borderless birth in a language she didn't yet speak.
She must have been so lonely, so confused. I try to remember this.
Though I'm so tired of empathy, itself a loneliness.
My mother who cries at a pecan tree's generous canopy,
but who could not cry for me, my ungenerous body.
What beauty have I ever held? Or held for long enough?
I chose none of it and receive none of it back.
Not birth, not country.
Like my mother, I chose to keep what was unplanned.
Though, I would love it.
I loved that not-body on the floor. The terrible clots.
Mother, I was the pecan tree. Briefly.
Until they scooped away my too-soft fruit,
my rot.

I HAVE NOTHING TO SHOW FOR MY POSTPARTUM BODY

Still, I carry the weight.
I hoist myself into the luxury SUV we bought *for safety.*
Still, I bleed. Like premium gas, I waste.
I sleep on the couch with the dogs for a week.
I cannot bear to be touched. I cut
off my hair with kitchen shears, stuff
what falls away into my fist.
I think about sewing the hair into a doll—
some unnatural thing. Proxy baby.
Instead, I throw the hair away.
Superstitions be damned.
Let someone make me into their black spell.
In this grief, I am golem,
eating marshmallow fluff by the spoonful.
My teeth protest, but I am trying to carve
my own hollow. One I consent to.
When I finally move back into our bed,
the father puts his hand on my still-swollen belly:
It still feels like you have a baby in there.
I turn on the TV. I pray for white noise.
There isn't any left. No static to fall into. No more stars.
Only a light too bright for my eyes.
That hand on my belly.
The emptiness.
The weight.

THERE ARE SEVEN CACTUS SPINES INSIDE MY PALMS, AND SO I MUST BE HOLY

The man I loved wants to kill me—
is this holiness? It's almost Christmas, and I'm shopping for a handgun.
When God impregnated Mary, he first sent an angel.
The angel Gabriel—like a Glock, almost. Announcing
the coming of Christ for at least one man.
Only here, there are no starry fields. No flocks. No shepherds.
All of the people in the park with purposeless herding dogs—
every one of them missing a perfect planetary alignment.
What a wiseman on the street corner points to and calls *the light show*.
The planet Venus, and all that.
Every dog is only some dominion to lord over.
Little darling promised lands, little ruined gardens. How stupidly
they read the ground. How stupidly I pray, too.
To the angel Gabriel, maybe. The time is right.
He comes in a dream. Like the man I loved—armed.

GUILT I

In the same dream,
Death walks off the tarot card face.
If Death is a woman, I cannot tell.
Still, I am not afraid—
and so, Death cannot be a man.
Death asks why I did not light a candle
in the hospital chapel.
Though I meant to.
Or let a balloon, as a white man told me to.
To get trapped in some atmospheric layer, I guess.
A grief that pollutes.
The whitest grief.
Death's hands are made of feathers. Not bone.
I picked them off every floor before I bled.
My baby was the bird I did not shoo quickly enough from my house.
My body the bad luck broom that swept it into some corner.
Dark and growing darker—scarlet
as sin. No, I could not attend the seventh day mass,
as my grandmother would have me.
What seventh day flowers were there to gather,
to watch wilt?

GUILT II

I could not follow Death, her birdsong.
Her leftover matter from the creation of the universe,
its infinite expanding and contracting—a womb.

Death was not a bad guest, but still, I tucked
a broom behind the door and sent her on her way.
Still, I lit Santa Muerte candles and spread chrysanthemums
on a three-tiered altar.

What is Death but another beloved?
A holy spirit? The other side of prayer?

I swept Death from the house
because I knew her breath
behind my ear to be my own,
and if I were to turn and look into her face,
I would find only a mirror.
Because I wanted her arms around me,
and she always was
out of reach.

THE UNHAUNTED POEM

X-Files child, I
        always wanted to brush

up against the paranormal.
        Grant me a final girl foggy day.

Though, in this only and on-
        forever life, I never found any ghost

outside the mirror. Only bare fruit trees
        controlled burns, abandoned hives, their capped

and long-dry combs. Only strangers
        with cheeks I kiss out of obligation,

not gentleness. Their go-with-God eyes
        betraying no glint of recognition,

no inheritance. This is only some memory
        or some photograph—whichever. A sign

neither of us can read for the other
        in such stale monolingual hallways.

The only language our proximity
        to Death, her sour chrysanthemum mouth.

See, when my Tia tells it, the dis-
        embodied hand in her bed shook

her until she woke, screaming.
        And for my father, then barefoot and dust-

rubbed boy, the ghost was only a hammock
		-hung daydream. A warning he felt—but not really.

A ghost, after all, is only a man.
		It saves its violence for women.

YEAH, I'M LATE TO WATCHING AHS 1984, BUT IT'S THE NIGHT TERRORS OF YOU MAKING GOOD ON YOUR PROMISE TO KILL ME THAT HAUNT ME

On-screen The Killer is any active shooter
white boy with greasy hair, and I'm bored.
In the dream your hands are very large.
It's 3 AM, and I'm on the phone with 24/7 customer support
just to talk to someone. No, because you reactivated
our Streaming Service™, and it overdrafted my account.
And the always-insomnia. How uninteresting,
all of this. The unchanged password regret.
A dream of Antarctica and not a single penguin.
Only freezing to death. Yes, I am lonely and can't sleep naked alone.
I got thousands in my pockets, you said.
How much money you working with?
I still purge when there isn't food in the fridge.
Maybe that answers your question.
See, a child draws a parent with large hands
when they're being abused. I was never
bruised, but you've made your threats.
Shan asks if you could be bluffing.
I've never been kind enough to lie. I need friends to feel concern—
when they find my body there won't be all this whodunnit.
Spare me the hour-long premiere;
save my only eternal soul from a 10-episode season.
A butterfly is powerful because it eats shit and dies.
But not before it crosses every border.
I'm just trying to cross over the curtain—or
maybe I've given up suicidality.
Paddington Bear feeds me marmalade
and teaches me the word for rain. Lluvia.
A sunshower in Portuguese is a fox's wedding.
No, it's o casamento da mariposa.

A pun is also a nightmare, see?
Anyway, they say wanting to die exists on a spectrum, now.
God's promise was a rainbow.
Your door-door idiots think it was the dove.
The sprig of olive. Ultralight beam.
Dumbass, the ghosts are already here.
God, His throwaway son. My cat pins them against the glass.
My superstitious ass can't stand a soul in flight.
Showing off, showing up, showing out.
I'm already damned
for accepting His bread-body on my unsaved tongue.
Child-me always dreamt of drowning
and wet the bed. All because two secular bastards
never sprinkled water on my head as an infant.
The passport photos were tough enough.
Give me your wailing birthright citizen baby.
Restrain her for her Documents.
This part is not a dream: you wanted me to join a cult.
Beyond the cult of this country, I mean.
When I said I wanted to die I didn't mean I wanted you to kill me.
Yeah, I'm a fucking rainbow. Bent beam of light.
Refracted promise. *Lying dyke*—
your words. Your large hands. I loved
your forearms, most. Tattoos in Old English.
A street talk secret: the gun violent
are first victims of gun violence. Anyway,
we'll always have our hatred of White America.
You, joining The Nation. Me, on my knees,
throwing up this cracked porcelain country.
What name have you chosen, Brother?
What should I call you when you come armed?
You will call me whitey. Not lover, not beloved.
Death To. I guess I asked for this.
My fish-eye lens anxiety, my still-beating heart.
You said you were a serial killer—I didn't listen.
Felonious. I tilted my head towards its outlaw music.
In the end, Satan was a woman, so play me out.
Here comes the synthwave, and there I go—
lifeless and most-beautiful.

POEM IN WHICH I TRY TO EAT FLAVORLESS SOUP AT PANERA AND INSTEAD LEAVE THREATENING TO PULL A GUN ON THE WHITE MAN WHO FOLLOWS ME TO MY CAR

The tomato soup tastes like "America"
if it tastes like anything at all. I wanted rabada—Dad's,
with mandioca, onions (green and sweet, both), cilantro
and the bode peppers he always got through customs, somehow.
On Twitter, Joaquin says, *You can't know a con artist and love one.*
And I think, *I love so many Brazilians.*
My father's only point of pride: my haggling,
my shit-talking, and, yes, my conning.
Every game of dominoes I took with drunk ease.
And then, the long con of it: this ALL LIVES MATTER country.
Shapeless thing made into some conflation
of two continents: "America." One country erasing
mine and how many others? How many Mexicos exist
in the white imagination? "Remember The Alamo" and forget the rest.
I will not honor some treaty signed under some Texas tree
by a general in white pants. When they teach us his name,
they do not even teach us half of it—like God, like country.
Generalísimo
Antonio de Padua María Severino López de Santa Anna y Pérez de Lebrón,
you could have stepped on Sam Houston's supine neck.
They cannot proffer receipts
for what was stolen (e.g., my rapist, never taken to court).
I'm sorry to tell you: this country is mine, too.
Its violence. Its guns. Mine, mine.
Its gnashing, course-correcting bullets—
their points hallowed as I am. I wear and tear at its skin:
I starve myself into white submission, unwillingly.
Yes, I like the hand around my throat—until I don't.
This country a lover that asks, *Are you okay? Did you like it?*

But never, *Can you breathe?*
How many times have I held the .357?
How straight and terrible my aim? True.
And still, white men land-and-pussy grab, unbothered.
Unbloodied.
And the trees now walk in silence, tired of our metallic mouths.
Root-first, they move towards water or a planet without us.

CORPUS DELICTI

Even as I say I can't absolve
that blue flag you fly
against softness,
I dial the number.
It was never the flag
I objected to—
whatever. We all claim
the imaginary lines
we were born into,
the empty clips.

Do the aunties still ask
if I called you
that unutterable slur
in bed—
as if lights and sirens
were a fantasy
and not abject terror,
as if every tattoo
was an oyster
and not a wound, scrawling
grave marker?

What I'm saying is,
I was the one who wanted
to name the baby Malcolm
or Hampton, but then,
that doesn't matter, anymore.
You can't tattoo
a name without a body.
The irony: a love-grief
like a courtroom.

When you don't answer,
I buy the discounted
olive tree slumped
a little in the shade.
Funny how our tethers find us.
Not a foil but a mirror
with its rib-ache posture
bad as mine,
resigned. I drive
with its branches
fruitless and dog-faced
out the window.

Home, past the single mariachi,
the couple kissing next to him
at the bus stop. Imagine,
the most unforgivable thing
being the first:
that you wouldn't kiss me.
I'm not interested
in defining what's criminal,
but there it is. A somehow-
somber accordion,
unaccompanied.

AFTER YOUR COUSIN WON'T LET ME HOLD THE BABY AT THE COOKOUT

I feel the baby falling out of me again. In clumps. Bleeding ash.
All tissue, no teeth. Deep red well water buried
and untapped. No witching rod. No witch. Nothing is divine
or left to divine. Maybe the crow is just a crow.
And the hawk just talons and hunt—not clarity of vision.
Only tunnel. Only eventual collapse.
What am I waiting to crash up against if not God? Me,
with my skin whiter than the teeth I grind and spit into a pulp nest.
As pollinator I am all hurt. Wicked and unapologetic.

    You will not forget me. No,

I didn't bear you a son. My blood like a bad circuit board or two poles
with the wrong charge. The white doctor inside me said *total abortion*,
and I wished for my great-grandmother, instead. Benzedeira.
If loss is actual, how much care is psychic?
Lullabies sung inside a skull to a swollen internal organ;
a forgotten tonic for grief; all things turning to brass; a body
that should have held two hearts but didn't.
Instead, the familiar arrhythmia and a new rush of blood—
but worse than blood.

    Our bodies are singing inside. I didn't know.

The ultrasound confirms it: our hollows are music.

How empty a glass.
How water makes it sing.
How wine.
How blood and body.

    Ah, but Lover and rib-shy of perfect equal,

your faith doesn't keep The Holy Spirit.
And my ancestors, what they kept in the dark,
scare you. What I keep, still.
The crucifix on the wall.
My Black Madonna Mother Country.
Yes, I can say a prayer and a curse at any crossroad.
Spill blood and spit fermented cane on any soil.
Bind or release you. Summon any spirit—
as many as you can think, plus one.
There is no death, only return.
No ghosts only gods.
My father prays after every lightning flash, and so I do.
Here, prayer is thanks. Never an ask.
We are saying Thank You because when they came for us,
we coded our faith into our bodies.
Because when they came for us, we danced.
We keep the light: feather-bright and smelted ore.
Storm and glory, I am not unholy—
but I am not unhaunted, either.

    Yes, I will carry your cells—always.

    Yes, my body is still a church.

Relic, reliquary, I walk away on the pads of my feet.

Not a trace left behind.

NOTES

Flood warning: "part of rib" and "piece of foreskin" refer to two types of relics. First, the ribs taken from the incorruptible bodies of saints such as St. Peregrine, St. Anthony and St. Nicholas. Second, the most-coveted relic, the holy foreskin, allegedly the foreskin saved from Christ's circumcision, now lost to the world. "I don't walk barefoot" is an allusion to St. Francis of Assisi, the barefoot saint.

Reliquary: "Not mosquito, not mosquito eater" refers to the common misclassification of the harmless crane fly. "Person not to possess" is a felony charge for anyone already convicted of a felony caught in possession of a firearm.

If the neighbors seem friendly it's only because they assume we are the same: This poem is indebted to Emily Mohn-Slate's "I am trying to write a joyful poem" (*The Falls,* New American Press, 2020). "No promise of rest in desolation" alludes to the apocryphal verse Esdras 1:58: "Until the land has enjoyed her sabbaths, she shall rest in her desolation."

There is only grief: "Six men lynched" speaks to the public lynchings across the country in tandem with the mass uprisings against police, Summer 2020. "I cannot tell a lie" alludes to Arlo Guthrie's refrain in the 1967 protest anthem and subsequent 1969 film, "Alice's Restaurant." Arlo's grandfather, Charley, was a member of the 40-man lynch mob that kidnapped and hung Laura and L.D. Nelson, mother and son, on May 25, 1911 in Okfuskee County, Oklahoma.

Poem for my immigrant father who has now left and will not come back: "a bird snare, a swarm of angry bees" is indebted to Amazonian tribes' indigenous language descriptions of the constellation Crux. The Kurâ (Bakairi) saw a bird snare; the Kalapalo saw bees emerging from the hive of the nearby Coalsack Nebula.

Watching "Lone Star Law" during the government shutdown over the border wall: "Lone Star Law" is an Animal Planet reality series (2016-present) that follows Texas game wardens as they police the state. "Your fingernails left in the mud like rosary beads" is indebted to the artist Tom Kiefer, who photographs the personal objects confiscated from migrants by CBP/ICE agents.

My father knows what work is: This poem is inspired in part by Philip Levine's *What Work Is* (Alfred A. Knopf, 1991). The closing image owes a debt of gratitude to Daniel Peña and his debut *Bang: a novel*, which sent a bolt of lightning through my brain and radically changed my craft. Thank you, Dan, for the gift of highlighting our shared cultural experience across the diaspora in something as small-but-profound as salting our oranges. Thank you for writing us, for us.

Gemini Baby: "it is a broken window world" invites criticism of the discredited criminological Broken Window Theory that ignores white supremacy's responsibility for structural racism, etc. "One man takes a knee for you" is an ode to Colin Kaepernick.

Poem in which I go to three different grocery stores in search of azeite de dende, only to spend $9 on a jar at the health foods store: "Not City of God but Stay With God" mentions, in part, the 2002 film by "Cidade de Deus." "What is *order* and *progress*" alludes to the slogan on the Brazilian flag "ordem e progresso." "What terrible math made me?" is indebted to Shannon Sankey's "I do a terrible math" from her poem "Hair" (*We Ran Rapturous*, The Atlas Review, 2019).

Poem about police violence: takes its title and quotes from June Jordan's poem "Poem about police violence," that famously asks "Tell me something / what you think would happen if / everytime they kill a black boy / then we kill a cop / everytime they kill a black man / then we kill a cop" (*Passion*, Beacon Press, 1980). Jordan wrote the poem after the 1978 murder of Arthur Miller, choked to death by police in Brooklyn, New York. This poem asks the same question, written after Officer Rusten Sheskey tased, assaulted and shot Jacob Blake, age 29, in Kenosha, Wisconsin on August 23, 2020. Sheskey has since returned to regular duty after a brief paid administrative leave. Jacob Blake survived, but he remains paralyzed. His children were seated in his car when Sheshkey opened fire. "My phone screen is still the precinct on fire" alludes to the Minnesota precinct set aflame after George Floyd was murdered by J. Alexander Kueng, Thomas Lane and Derek Chauvin. "Cobalt will have you crazy in a cornfield, we already know" is an allusion to Picasso.

5-O Radio: 5-O Radio is a downloadable police scanner app. "Would that they would bloat and float away across the ocean. Let them be the raft, one time" laments all refugee lives lost to the ocean, as informed by the Cuban refugees of my 90s childhood. Antwon Rose, age 17, was murdered by Officer Michael Rosfeld while fleeing police in Pittsburgh, Pennsylvania's Hill District, June 19, 2018. Rosfeld was acquitted of all charges.

Before the raids begin, I drive to work with a mango in my lap: "ataulfo or Tommy Atkins/ Haden— / the latter mangoes I have to Google to name. All fiber and long shelf life. / Named for white men in Florida" speaks to the colonial history/violence of mango cultivation. "*Animal*" is italicized to emphasize the hate speech that encouraged acts of violence against immigrants in regular use by the U.S.' fascist 45th president, Donald Trump. "Red light. They will come for us..." speaks to the sweeping ICE raids across the country under Trump. "Having sliced open their own palms" refers to the phenomenon of Europeans slicing open their palms while unsuccessfully trying to open avocados—a headline with its own post-colonial poetic justice. "Always, Once or Still, white men sell human fat as a delicacy" refers to the common practice of selling human fat for consumption after guillotine executions. *Removed* is italicized to highlight a troubling change in immigration policy rhetoric: after 1997, deportation proceedings were referred to as "removal proceedings" under the Illegal Immigration Reform and Immigrant Responsibility Act of 1996. "Every mango left heavy on the branch" refers to the mangoes left unpicked due to the labor and subsequent produce shortages in the U.S. after sweeping ICE raids, immigrant detention and deportations under Trump. Never forget who feeds this country.

Before the blood, I only know you through a screen: As of the printing of this book, more than half of U.S. states (26) require a person to be subjected to an ultrasound before allowing abortion procedures. "As if Triangle Trade didn't hit us hardest:" Brazil imported more kidnapped and enslaved Africans (an estimated 4.9 million) than any other country, and is subsequently the country with the largest Black population outside of Africa. Nossa Senhora da Conceição Aparecida, the Black Madonna, is our patron saint. In spite of the fact that Brazilian culture and Brazil itself would not exist without Afro Brazilians, colonialism's legacy of anti-Blackness persists.

People say the world has always been breaking around us: This poem was written in response to the armed white supremacist militias patrolling the U.S./Mexico border, with Trump inciting them to "shoot [migrants] in the kneecaps." (Unsurprisingly, Joe Biden later used the same language of "shooting them in the kneecaps" to order police violence.) The poem imagines a world in which immigrants are able to express our rage—and act on it/in self defense—as openly as white U.S. citizens/white nationalists are able to enact terrorism through their racism and xenophobia. "How can a train be a beast / when no white man will slaughter it, / leaving us to starve / and it belly-up and wasted / on red hills?" refers to the U.S. settler colonial state's systematic campaign to starve Great Plains tribes by eradicating their food source, the American bison, in order to eject natives from their lands and onto reservations. "Mother Desert will not abide / her buzzards // to carry cowards / into ascension" draws from many indigenous desert cultures' belief that carrion birds carry our spirits to the sun/heaven. "And though The Rebel From Nazareth / said to wet mine enemies' lips" draws from Proverbs 25:21-22. ("If your enemy is hungry, give him food to eat; And if he is thirsty, give him water to drink.") This poem mentions United We Dream's MigraWatch app, which is free to download, and helps protect the community against ICE raids and agents.

If I were to write my Latinx novel, I simply would not: Together with "Wire," this poem was written in outrage against *American Dirt* (Flatiron Books, 2018). "Itself a mutation—a mother's cursed privilege / first appearing in a single individual / only 7,000 years ago" cites the evolutionary biology that tells us pale skin arrived relatively recently in human history as a genetic anomaly (here as an argument against white supremacy). *"Reunification… removal"* refers to the "immigration policy" optics that claimed to end family separation at the border—even as migrants remain in detention or disappeared. "Not apple but pomegranate" refers to the common misperception of the Biblical forbidden fruit as an apple. While the apple is not original to the Hebrew Bible, which never specified the fruit, it can be traced back to a Latin pun (malus: evil/apple) made in translation by the fourth century scholar Jerome and popularized by Milton.

To the white woman who thought a palo santo stick was a useless decorative object while her sisters drive the plant into extinction and The Amazon still burns: Rest in power, Paulo Paulino Guajajara, indigenous forest guardian and land steward murdered by illegal loggers in Arariboia, Brazil on November 1, 2019. Between 2000 and 2018, 42 Guajajara Indigenous People were murdered by invaders. Chief Raoni Metuktire is chief of the Kayapó people and a climate justice warrior. He famously made contact with the outside world to appeal for protections for the land, its people. Jair Bolsonaro is the 38th president of Brazil who ran and won on an intensely pro-industry, anti-indigenous peoples platform. Chief Raoni, now almost 100 years old, called Bolsonaro "the worst" president for indigenous peoples in Brazil. "This country: all parking lots and The Seventh Cavalry opening fire. / The irony. Declaring The Badlands public land" connects the violent anti-indigeneity across both countries, Brazil and the U.S. It alludes to the massacre of Lakota people at Wounded Knee by The Seventh Cavalry as the Lakota fled for The Badlands (now a "National Park"). LAND BACK.

In which the poem always contains a shark and never a baby: "Nothing remained but a complicated sadness— / because inside sadness you can arrive at relief" owes a debt of gratitude to Emily Mohn-Slate's line "Joy must be at least / as complicated as sorrow" from "I'm trying to write a joyful poem" (*The Falls,* New American Press, 2020).

What wasn't gathered: "How many lemmings did scientists throw from how many cliffs?" refers to the common misconception that lemmings leap from cliffs in mass suicide. Rather, lemmings purchased from Native children were thrown from cliffs by filmmakers for the 1958 Disney production "White Wilderness."

I have nothing to show for my postpartum body: "I turn on the TV. I pray for white noise. / There isn't any left. No static to fall into. No more stars" pulls from the scientific theory that analog TV static interprets cosmic microwave background leftover from the Big Bang.

Guilt I: "Dark and growing darker—scarlet / as sin" alludes to Isaiah 1:18 ("Though your sins be as scarlet"). Brazilian Catholicism still maintains the "Requiem Mass," or mass for the dead, on the seventh day for the repose of the soul.

Guilt II: To place a broom behind a door is to keep away evil spirits and unwanted guests, or to get rid of existing guests. Chrysanthemums are reserved for funerals and associated with keeping the dead.

Yeah, I'm late to watching AHS 1984, but it's the night terrors of you making good on your promise to kill me that haunt me: American Horror Story 1984 premiered in 2019 on FX. "Anyway, they say wanting to die exists on a spectrum, now" was inspired by the transformative 2019 *The Outline* article by Anna Borges, "I am not always very attached to being alive." "God's promise was a rainbow. / Your door-door idiots think it was the dove" refers to the flood in Genesis. It's both an allusion to Elizabeth Bishop's poem "The Fish" and a celebration of queerness. "Ultralight beam" is, of course, an allusion to Kanye West's gospel-infused song from the 2016 album, *Life of Pablo*. "Tattoos in Old English" alludes to The Game's song "Ol' English" from the 2006 album *Doctor's Advocate*.

Poem in which I try to eat flavorless soup at Panera and instead leave threatening to pull a gun on the white man who follows me to my car: Thank you Joaquin Fernandez for permission to quote his Tweet here. "I will not honor some treaty signed under some Texas tree / by a general in white pants" is an allusion to the 1886 painting by William Henry Huddle, "Surrender of Santa Anna," which is hung on display at the Texas State Capitol. The general was made to wear a private's white pants as an act of humiliation. Together with ""Remember The Alamo" and forget the rest," the poem criticizes the white supremacist lens through which Texas history is taught on this stolen land. The poem and its line "And still, white men land-and-pussy grab" connect colonialist/imperialist violence against the land-as-matriarch to violence against women (alluding to Donald Trump publicly lauding sexual assault).

Corpus delicti: "Corpus delicti" is a legal term that dictates a "crime" must be proven to have taken place in order for a person to be convicted of said crime. E.g., theoretically a person could not be convicted of murder without a body. "You can't tattoo / a name without a body. / The irony: a love-grief / like a courtroom" pulls from this.

After your cousin won't let me hold the baby at the cookout: A benzedeira is a Brazilian folk healer or medicine woman. "Ah, but Lover and rib-shy of perfect equal," subverts the Christian patriarchal tradition by re-positioning women as more powerful than (i.e. not less-than) men (in a return to matriarchy). "We are saying thank you" is an ode to W.S. Merwin. This poem alludes to Candomblé and other ancestral spiritual practices/faiths, as well as celebrating capoeira: "because when they came for us, / we coded our faith into our bodies. / Because when they came for us, we danced." Faith is the diaspora's resistance.

This text relies on a certain level of understanding of branqueamento, Latin America's white supremacist project to "correct" its peoples' Blackness and indigeneity by miscegenation. Most acutely when asking "what terrible math made me," in "Poem in which I go to three different grocery stores in search of azeite de dende, only to spend $9 on a jar at the health foods store," this text's thesis—in conversation with Malcolm Friend's poem, "Dispersion Theory: Polynegro," which demands:

"Telling the Americas' post-racial voices
we will never imagine
a future without Blackness."

I recognize this knowledge base may not be immediately available to a U.S. audience, who is consequently invited to look to Modesto Brocos Gómez's 1895 oil painting, "Redenção de Cam," for a succinct depiction of the problem.

PREVIOUS PUBLICATIONS

A previous version of "Flood warning" was published in *HitchLit Review*'s *Secular Special: Women's Voices* issue.

"There is only grief" was published in *PANK! Magazine*'s Latinx Lit Celebration.

"Poem for my immigrant father, who has now left and will not come back" was published in *Borderlands: Texas Poetry Review*.

"Watching "Lone Star Law" during the government shutdown over the border wall" was published in *Glass: a Journal of Poetry*'s Poets Resist series.

"Animals" was published in *Pidgeonholes*.

"My father knows what work is" was published in *The Missouri Review* as a Poem of the Week web feature.

"Gemini Baby," "What wasn't gathered" and "To the white woman who thought a palo santo stick was a useless decorative object while her sisters drive the plant into extinction and the Amazon still burns" were all published in *EcoTheo Review*. "Gemini Baby" was nominated for Best of the Net 2020.

"5-O Radio" and "There are seven cactus spines inside my palms, and so I must be holy" were published in *Best Buds! Collective*.

The full version of "Before the raids begin, I drive to work with a mango in my lap" was published in *Duende*.

"If I were to write my Latinx novel, I simply would not" and "Wire" were published in *Hinchas de Poesia*.

"Devotion" was published in *No Tender Fences: an Anthology of Immigrant and First-Generation American Poetry*.

"In which the poem always contains a shark and never a baby" was published in *PALABRITAS*.

"Caracol" was published in *The Boiler*.

"The unhaunted poem" was published in *Heavy Feather Review's* Haunted Passages.

"Yeah, I'm late to watching AHS 1984, but it's the night terrors of you making good on your promise to kill me that haunt me" was published in *Drunk Monkey's* Rad Ass! Pop Culture Issue and nominated for Best of The Net 2020.

"Poem in which I try to eat flavorless soup at Panera and instead leave threatening to pull a gun on the white man who follows me to my car" was first published in *The Bayou Review* in a surprise admission by Dan Peña.

IN GRATITUDE

For Boosie. We did it.

For Azad Amir Smith, who will always loom large as the blue lines drawn through the city of Pittsburgh. Thank you for seeing and holding me. You say militant, I say radical. Together, we are revolutionaries. Essa eu fiz com você.

For my family. Thank you, Dad, for the incredible act of your border crossings—for everything you made possible. Nada tema! Thank you, Mom, for the gift of two places, two worlds. And to every far-flung Sousa. What a gift to be so loved across such a distance, diaspora.

For my Dindinha, a woman I never met, but whom I carry with me. She haunts me in this life and in these pages. I hope I wear your witch's mark well. Thank you for loving and protecting me.

For Shannon Sankey, forever my first reader and most-brilliant poet- and curl-friend. Thank you for being a friend across the table and in this life. I love you, sqrl.

For my Pittsburgh heroes: Emily Mohn-Slate, Malcolm Friend and Dan Shapiro. Thank you all for being such forces of good in that city—and for being such fierce supporters and friends. You each have a forever hype man in me. Emily, I would not be a poet, this would not be a book, without your tenderness and support. Thank you for giving me permission to value and trust in myself, my work. And thank you for being there for me through loss. I love you, and the Mohn-Slate crew, to the moon and back.

For Jennifer Jackson Berry who encouraged me to write about miscarriage. Thank you for sharing in this work and healing with me.

For every person who has experienced pregnancy loss and gone on, in spite of. For learning to carry this worry stone grief.

For my comrades Mark Cugini and Jorge Gomez, who both paid my contest submission fees for me, making this book possible, and who are both consistently in my corner. Thank you both for always doing the work to uplift the people around you.

For the dream of a more equitable arts world. Poetry belongs to the people; the people are working class; poetry belongs to the working class. Long may we honor, tend and keep the oral traditions of our ancestors.

For my extended Latinx fam: thank you to everyone online and IRL who I've been privileged enough to make a meaningful connection with. Extra special shout to Jorge Gomez (again!), C.T. Salazar and Juan Ochoa for inviting my poems into their classrooms—what a gift! And to Alan Chazaro, my poetry primo. Thank you for your trust, your friendship and your work; it's an honor to undertake it with you. I will always be in awe of your hustle.

For Kelly Mendiola, Doug Dorst and Alan Altimont, who encouraged me to write before I considered myself a writer. Dr. Altimont, thank you for your suspicion that I was a poet—it was, and sometimes still is, a surprise to me. I can point precisely to where it clicked: your essay writing class in France. How wonderfully surreal.

For Stefanie Wielkopolan, Pat Hart, Rob Nichols and Helena Ache: thank you for being my first workshop group in Pittsburgh—and my favorite ever. Walking to the neighborhood coffee shop from my spare first apartment to meet with you will always be a favorite memory from that city. All of us ordinary people, celebrating the work.

To *The Pittsburgh Post-Gazette, Rogue Agent, PEN America & The Rattling Wall* and *Poet Lore* for being my first publications and for believing in early work. Encouragement is such a gift. For Jody Bolz at *Poet Lore*, especially, for her careful attention to my first in-print poem.

For the city of Pittsburgh, where I became a poet. Thank you for fueling the fire, for giving me a community. I hope the city's future brings more justice, more peace and a more equitable tomorrow. Never forget who built you, who claims and sings you—and who you turn your back on.

For White Whale Bookstore: thank you for being our community's pulse. You do so much invaluable work for the city of Pittsburgh, and it's truly a better place because of you. Thank you, too, for helping us hold space for protest with Writers for Migrant Justice. I truly could not have done it without you, and I am still humbled by how the city showed up that night. It was a perfect send off from Pittsburgh.

For Writers for Migrant Justice. Thank you to Adriana Ramírez and Tanya Shirazi for lending your voices to the cause at our all-Latinx Pittsburgh chapter. Malcolm, thank you for being on board before the thing even had a shape. Emily, thank you for encouraging me to Act. Thank you to everyone across the United States who demanded an end to migrant detention with us that night. And, of course, a standing ovation for Christopher Soto, Javier Zamora, Jan-Henry Gray and Anni Liu for bringing us together across time and space to effect change.

For immigrant and migrant advocacy networks like Immigrant Families Together and RAICES Texas. Thank you for all your labor to protect the most vulnerable among and on their way to us. May we see the abolition of borders, their violence, in our lifetime. May every crossing be safe and swift—and every dream realized.

For Black Lives Matter and grassroots organizers for liberation—in the U.S. and beyond. A powerful protection circle around you all. None of us are free until we are all free.

For accountability projects like Mapping Police Violence and Cultural Survival: Advancing Indigenous Peoples Rights & Cultures Worldwide and the American Immigration Lawyers Association.

For Rodríguez Calero, "RoCa," for her art, and for her permission to use "The Blessing of Lazarus" for this book's cover.

For John Freeman and the Academy of American Poets' permission to use lines from Freeman's poem "Saudade" (originally published in Poem-a-Day on October 10, 2017) as this book's epigraph.

And, finally, for the poets. My heroes. So many poets have informed my poetry, my conception of myself as a poet; here named are just a few of my dearest: Elizabeth Bishop, Jericho Brown, Melanie Braverman, Lucille Clifton, Roque Dalton, Carolyn Forché, Juan Felipe Herrera, June Jordan, W.S. Merwin, Carl Phillips, Claudia Rankine, Charles Simic, Solmaz Sharif, A.E. Stallings, C.D. Wright, Ocean Vuong.

For Ross Gay, especially, whose work made this book possible. Your interview on Rachel Zucker's podcast, *Commonplace: Conversations with Poets*, wherein you talked about the long poem allowing more life, more messiness in, broke open my process. I wrote "Poem for my immigrant father who has now left and will not come back" immediately after listening to your words. That poem was the start of this manuscript. I work every day to cultivate joy-as-resistance by your example, radiant poet.

And for rage. May we never quiet it—it shows us the way to a more-possible world.

Photo: Emily Sousa

Kim Sousa (she/they) is a queer Brazilian American poet and open border radical. She was born in Goiânia, Goiás and immigrated to Austin, Texas with her family at age five. In 2019, Kim organized and participated in Pittsburgh's all-Latinx chapter of Christopher Soto, et al.'s Writers for Migrant Justice nation-wide protest reading series, which benefited Immigrant Families Together. Alongside Carla Ferreira, she also co-edited the limited run benefit anthology of immigrant and first-generation poetry, *No Tender Fences*, which donated 100% of its proceeds to RAICES Texas. Kim is the editor of *Até Mais: Until More, an Anthology of Latinx Futurisms* (forthcoming Deep Vellum Publishing) with Malcolm Friend and Alan Chazaro. You can find her at kimsousawrites.com and on Twitter @kimsoandso.

ALWAYS A RELIC NEVER A RELIQUARY is Kim's first book.

www.ingramcontent.com/pod-product-compliance
Lightning Source LLC
LaVergne TN
LVHW081528060526
838200LV00045B/2039